AMERICA'S ETHNIC DIVERSITY

ASIAN AMERICANS

by Keng Xiong

BrightPoint Press

San Diego, CA

BrightPoint Press

an imprint of ReferencePoint Press, Inc.
Printed in the United States

For more information, contact:
BrightPoint Press
PO Box 27779
San Diego, CA 92198
www.BrightPointPress.com

LIBRARY OF CONGRESS CATALOGING-IN-PUBLICATION DATA

Names: Xiong, Keng, author.
Title: Asian Americans / by Keng Xiong.
Description: San Diego, CA: BrightPoint Press, [2026] | Series: America's ethnic diversity | Includes bibliographical references and index. | Audience: Grades 7–9
Identifiers: LCCN 2024055837 (print) | LCCN 2024055838 (eBook) | ISBN 9781678210960 (hardcover) | ISBN 9781678210977 (eBook)
Subjects: LCSH: Asian Americans--Juvenile literature.
Classification: LCC E184.A75 X56 2026 (print) | LCC E184.A75 (eBook) | DDC 305.895/073--dc23/eng/20250203
LC record available at https://lccn.loc.gov/2024055837
LC eBook record available at https://lccn.loc.gov/2024055838

CONTENTS

AT A GLANCE

- Asian Americans are one of the fastest-growing racial minority groups in the United States.
- In 1763, Filipinos were the first Asians to arrive and settle in what is now the United States.
- In the 1850s, many Chinese immigrants came to California in search of gold and jobs. Asian immigrants often faced discrimination and laws that limited their opportunities.
- Asian Americans fought for their rights through boycotts and strikes alongside other people of color.
- Asian Americans have many different cultures and traditions, as well as religions and religious celebrations. Some may follow Christianity, Islam, Hinduism, Buddhism, or no religion.

- There are many ethnicities, or subgroups, of Asian Americans. They can be found across the United States and in different career paths.
- Asian Americans may often be grouped as a monolith and seen as model minorities.
- Asian/Pacific American Heritage Month is celebrated in May. It reflects on the diverse identities of Asian and Pacific Islander heritage.

A FESTIVE CELEBRATION

It was Aden's first time celebrating the Mid-Autumn Festival in New York City. Aden was born in America. But his family is Chinese. He was excited to explore the festival. He was going with a friend.

When Aden arrived, he saw a big crowd. The street was full of families enjoying the festival. Food and art booths lined the street. Aden could hear flute music. He smelled stinky tofu, a fermented tofu dish.

New York City's Mid-Autumn Festival celebration takes place in Chinatown. New York City's Chinatown is home to the largest group of Chinese people in the western hemisphere.

EYE SOLUTIONS
SCHOOL
SPEED LIMIT 20
212-285

Mooncakes are a traditional food at the Mid-Autumn Festival.

Some people wore traditional clothes. There were also colorful decorations and lanterns.

Far away, Aden heard the beat of a drum. Aden walked closer. He saw two dancers. They wore costumes that made them look like lions. They danced with the music.

The lion dancers held sticks of light. They swirled them through the darkness.

After the show, Aden and his friend got mooncakes. Mooncakes are sweet-savory pastries with different fillings. Some include egg yolks. Others have red-bean paste. They were delicious!

DIVERSE IDENTITIES

The United States is home to people from many ethnic groups. People in each ethnic group come from different countries or regions around the world. Each person has their own culture. And every person has their own identity. Diversity is the bringing together of different kinds of people. Diversity brings new ideas and understanding of different identities and backgrounds. It also shows how people are connected. Diversity gives people a chance to learn about other races, religions, and languages.

Asian Americans are part of that diversity. Americans with Asian heritage are Asian Americans. They may have been born in America. Or they may have **immigrated** to the United States. They may stay connected to their Asian cultures and traditions. They might also embrace American traditions. How each person incorporates these cultures into their lives is unique. They all have their own stories. Asian Americans are one of the fastest-growing racial minority groups in the United States.

Indian Americans celebrate Indian Independence Day (August 15) in New York City.

CHAPTER ONE

ASIAN AMERICAN HISTORY

The term *Asian American* did not always exist. It was coined by activists in 1968. Yuji Ichioka and Emma Gee were students at the University of California, Berkeley. They founded the Asian American Political Alliance. This was a community space where Asian Americans could come together.

Asian Americans may not have always used the term. But they have a long history

The University of California, Berkeley, launched an Asian American Research Center in 2020.

in the United States. Erika Lee is the author of *The Making of Asian America*. She writes, "The history of Asian Americans is also immigration history."[1]

THE FIRST ASIAN IMMIGRANTS

Filipinos were the first Asians in America. The Philippines was a Spanish colony. Filipino sailors were known as Manilamen. They brought goods to other Spanish colonies in the Caribbean Sea. Manilamen arrived in the United States in 1763. This was before the Revolutionary War (1775–1783). They settled in what is now Louisiana.

A new wave of Asian immigrants arrived in the 1850s. Many were Chinese. They came to California. Gold had been found at a mill in 1848. This discovery started the California Gold Rush. People came from all over. They hoped to find gold and become rich.

Some immigrants planned to return to their home countries. Others were refugees.

Manilamen created a settlement called Saint Malo along Lake Borgne in Louisiana. The town was destroyed by a hurricane in the early 1900s. Lake Borgne is also home to Fort Proctor (pictured).

The 155th anniversary of finishing the Transcontinental Railroad took place in 2024. The anniversary celebration included a moment of silence to honor railroad workers who lost their lives.

They were running from war and high taxes. They were looking for a safe place to live. About 25,000 Chinese immigrants had arrived by 1851.

Beginning in 1863, Chinese immigrants helped build the Transcontinental Railroad. This was the first railroad that went across the United States. It was completed in 1869.

Work conditions were harsh. The work was dangerous. Many Chinese people lost their lives.

As more Chinese immigrants came to the United States, they faced challenges. One was **discrimination**. American citizens worried immigrants would take their jobs. Some made **racist** remarks. Chinese **stereotypes** became common.

IMMIGRATION CONTROL

The US government also discriminated against Chinese immigrants. President Chester A. Arthur signed the Chinese Exclusion Act in 1882. The rule stopped Chinese workers from coming to the United States. Under this rule, Chinese immigrants could not apply for American citizenship.

That meant they couldn't have the same rights as other Americans. The rule lasted until 1943.

After the Chinese Exclusion Act, other Asian immigrants came to the United States. Many were Japanese. They arrived in San Francisco, California. Before entering the country, they had to be checked in. Immigrants to San Francisco stopped at Angel Island. Newcomers gave their names and home countries. They were separated by race and sex. They had to wait to be examined before entering the country. This included medical exams and long interviews. Sometimes they waited for days. Some even waited for years. The process was harsh. Immigrants were kept in small rooms. The place was like a prison.

In 1917, Congress passed a new law. It wanted to stop immigrants from coming to the United States. These included immigrants from Asia and Europe. The law kept most people born in the Asiatic Barred Zone from entering the country. This zone extended from the Middle East

Vincent Chin

On June 19, 1982, Vincent Chin was the victim of an anti-Asian **hate crime**. Chin was Chinese American. He worked in the car industry. The American car industry was suffering at the time. Many people blamed Japanese car companies. Ronald Ebens and Michael Nitz were white auto workers. They believed Chin was Japanese. They chased him and beat him to death. They did not go to jail. Chin's death brought many Asian American communities together in protest.

to Southeast Asia. Japanese people and Filipinos were exceptions to the barred zone. The Japanese government already limited Japanese immigrants going to the United States. And the Philippines was a US colony. This meant its people could travel back and forth. But other Asian immigrants couldn't legally enter the United States.

On December 7, 1941, Japanese soldiers bombed Pearl Harbor in Hawaii. This caused the United States to enter World War II (1939–1945). President Franklin D. Roosevelt forced more than 120,000 Japanese Americans into **confinement camps**. Many families were separated. They lost their homes and businesses. The camps were surrounded with barbed wire.

The Granada Relocation Center in Colorado was one of many confinement camps. The government forced Japanese Americans to live in these camps during World War II.

Armed guards stood watch. People lived in barracks. They slept on cots. The camps were disbanded by 1946. But many Japanese Americans were left without homes and jobs.

FIGHTING BACK

Asian Americans have faced discrimination throughout US history. But they have also come together to fight for their rights.

In 1965, the Agricultural Workers Organizing Committee (AWOC) led a work strike. More than 800 farmworkers with AWOC were Filipino Americans. They picked grapes in California. They wanted better pay and working conditions. The strike sparked an international **boycott** of table grapes. The strike lasted 5 years. The workers were successful. They got higher wages and safer working conditions.

In 1968, Asian American students went on strike. They studied at San Francisco State University. Asian Americans and other students of color wanted to change the education system. They wanted to add classes that reflected their own diverse identities. Protests lasted many months. They spread to UC Berkeley.

Student groups in the 1960s formed the Third World Liberation Front. This group led the student strikes of 1968.

There, protesters helped create the Department of Ethnic Studies.

Asian Americans play an important role in US history. They have faced discrimination. This discrimination continues today. But Asian Americans have fought for their rights. They have gained recognition for their important role throughout US history.

CHAPTER TWO

MANY CULTURES AND TRADITIONS

The term *Asian American* groups different ethnicities. People may trace their Asian heritage to multiple countries. Cultures and traditions may overlap. Some people follow them. Others may not.

EAST ASIAN AMERICANS

East Asia includes China, Japan, North Korea, and South Korea. Chinese Americans are the largest Asian American

Chinese Americans may celebrate Chinese New Year. This is a major Lunar New Year celebration. Others include Seollal in Korea and Tết in Vietnam.

百年好合

Dragon dances are a major part of many Chinese New Year celebrations.

ethnic group. There are more than 5 million Chinese Americans in the United States. They may celebrate traditions from Chinese heritage. One of these is the Spring Festival, also called Chinese New Year. It lasts for about 15 days and welcomes the spring. Families often gather to celebrate together. Children receive red paper envelopes. Money is inside. The envelopes are a symbol of good fortune for the year. There are also performances such as lion dances.

Justin Le belongs to the New York Chinese Freemasons Athletic Club. He is part of the lion dance troupe. He says, "I value my culture and tradition, being Chinese or Asian American. I have a lot of pride in that. . . . I want to contribute and give back to the community."[2]

More than 1 million Japanese Americans live in the United States. Japanese cultural traditions may center around family, education, and work. One Japanese festival is Sakura Matsuri. It is also called the Cherry Blossom Festival. Washington, DC, has a celebration every year. It happens when the cherry

Doljabi

Doljabi is a Korean fortune-telling tradition. It happens on a baby's first birthday. The baby is given different objects. These may include a pencil, a piece of thread, and money. They represent knowledge, a long life, and wealth. The baby chooses one. The choice is said to be a sign of their future.

trees bloom. People celebrate with folk songs and traditional dancing.

SOUTH ASIAN AMERICANS

South Asian countries include India, Pakistan, Nepal, and Bangladesh. There are more than 4 million Indian Americans. Pakistani Americans are the second-largest South Asian American group. Many South Asian traditions and beliefs stem from family. Some family elders may arrange marriages. Marriage joins two families together. Indian Americans often celebrate weddings with extended family. The bride may wear henna. This is a red-brown dye. It is applied to the hands and feet. The designs represent hopes for a happy marriage.

Indian wedding celebrations often last for several days.

Some traditions are not as positive. Many South Asian countries have a historic caste system. This is a social ranking system that people are born into. The system has been officially removed in many places. But it remains in the culture. Laurence Simon is a professor of international development. He says, "It appeared to me . . . that there was within the South Asian community an ongoing discrimination based on the attitudes that many people grow up with in the old countries."[3] These traditions can cause discrimination and **prejudice**.

SOUTHEAST ASIAN AMERICANS

Southeast Asia includes Thailand, the Philippines, and Vietnam. Filipino Americans are the largest Southeast

Asian American group. Filipino Americans celebrate Filipino Independence Day. On June 12, 1898, the Philippines gained freedom from Spain. Independence from the United States came in 1946. Since then, Filipinos across the world have celebrated. Some gather and have feasts. Popular foods include adobo and sinigang. Adobo is a stewed chicken or pork dish. Sinigang is a sour soup.

There are more than 2 million Vietnamese Americans. The Vietnamese New Year is an important cultural celebration. It is called Tết Nguyên Đán. The 3-day festival is often celebrated with loved ones. Vietnamese Americans may prepare holiday foods. Pork and eggs in a caramel sauce is a traditional dish. Vietnamese Americans may clean

People do not always agree on how to define regions. Afghanistan is considered by some to be in South Asia, by others to be in Central Asia or the Middle East.

ASIAN AMERICANS IN THE UNITED STATES

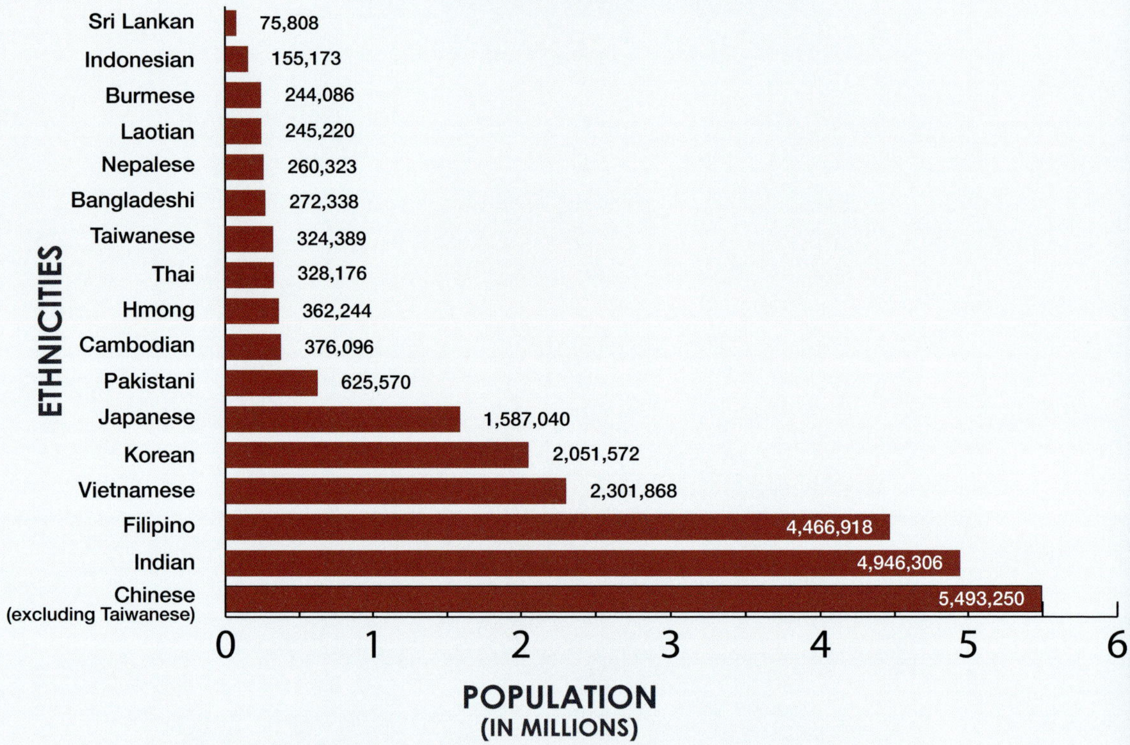

Source: US Census Bureau, "Selected Population Profile in the United States," American Community Survey, *2022, http://data.census.gov.*

The US Census Bureau estimates the populations of ethnic groups with more than 65,000 members. Because some people belong to more than one ethnic group, the numbers add up to more than the total Asian American population.

their homes to welcome the new year. Communities may also host events and performances. Some people wear ao dai.

This is traditional Vietnamese clothing. Thinh Dinh helps organize a Lunar New Year Festival. He says,

> *It's a time to remember our ancestors and get together with family. Here it can be isolating for Vietnamese, so it's a chance for them to come out and meet other Vietnamese and anyone else who wants to experience our culture.*[4]

Asian Americans have made their own celebrations and traditions in the United States. Many cultures and traditions exist within a country. They all play a part in Asian American culture.

CHAPTER THREE

ASIAN AMERICAN RELIGIONS AND CELEBRATIONS

Asian Americans may practice different religions. These include Christianity, Islam, Hinduism, and Buddhism. They may also practice other religions or no religion.

CHRISTIANITY

Christianity is the most-practiced religion in the world. It is monotheistic. This means Christians believe in one God. There are different branches of Christianity.

A Pew Research Center survey found that 34 percent of Asian Americans are Christian.

Most Asian American Christians are Catholic or Protestant. There are many ways to practice Christianity. People may go to church. They may sing praises to God. They may read from the Holy Bible.

Christmas is a popular holiday. It celebrates the birth of Jesus Christ. Families may gather. Sometimes they open presents. Easter is another Christian holiday. It celebrates Jesus Christ returning to life after he died on the cross.

ISLAM

Some Asian Americans practice Islam. Followers of Islam are called Muslims. They follow one God, called Allah. They often pray at mosques or Islamic centers. They may follow the five pillars of Islam.

These are core beliefs and practices. Mecca is a holy site. It is the home of the Prophet Muhammad. He is the founder of Islam. Many Muslims turn toward Mecca to pray. They may do this throughout the day. This prayer ritual is known as Salah. During prayer, Muslims recite verses from the Quran. This is the Muslim holy book.

Ramadan is an important Islamic tradition. It is known as the holy month

Shamanism

Some Asian Americans practice Shamanism. This is a spiritual practice centered around a shaman. A shaman acts as a medium between the physical and spiritual worlds. Shamans may heal sick people. They may provide answers during hard times.

Muslims may gather during Ramadan to break their fast together.

of fasting. Fasting means no eating or drinking. During Ramadan, Muslims often fast during the day. They break the fast at sunset. At the end of the month, Muslims may celebrate Eid al-Fitr. To break their fast, families and friends gather to share meals.

Ibrahim Nazir organized an Eid celebration in the United Kingdom. He explains that Ramadan is about more than fasting. “It’s not just the fast of food and drink, but also a training camp,” Nazir says. “So at the end of it you come out as a better human being and a better Muslim.”[5]

HINDUISM

Hinduism is a religion that began in India. It mainly follows one god, Brahma. But it also has other gods, known as deities. Hindus follow the Vedas. These are holy texts. Hindus may pray at temples. Temples are places of worship. Hindus may also pray to shrines at home. Hindus may believe in reincarnation. This is where someone’s soul is reborn in a different body after death. Hindus may also believe in karma. This is the belief that a person’s actions will affect their next life.

One Hindu holiday is Holi. This is the festival of colors. People often throw colored water and powders on each other. It is a day where social labels are ignored. These include age, caste, and gender. During Holi, everyone celebrates together. Diwali is another Hindu holiday. It is known as the

Holi takes place in the spring.

festival of lights. It lasts 5 days. People often celebrate with friends and family. They have large feasts. Diwali is sometimes celebrated in Buddhist cultures, too.

BUDDHISM

Buddhism is another common Asian religion. Buddhists follow the Buddha's teachings. These include the Four Noble Truths and the Eight-Fold Path. The teachings are a way to enlightenment. Enlightenment happens when a person can stop selfish desires. Buddhists may practice meditation and prayer. They may also believe in spirits, reincarnation, and karma.

Obon is a holiday celebrating the spirits of ancestors. People believe loved ones come back to visit their families.

Celebrants clean family gravestones and set out lanterns. Sometimes they place lanterns into the water. Performers may dance in traditional clothing. These performances are known as *bon odori*. They are meant to greet and send off spirits.

Asian Americans may believe in different religions. Some may not practice any. Dheepa Sundaram is a professor of religious studies. She says,

> *Religion does not mean the same thing to all people and is steeped in Western assumptions about faith and belief. For example, Chinese people rarely use the term "religion" to describe their beliefs and traditions or the language of belief to discuss their relationships with gods.*[6]

Buddha statues are symbols of the Buddha's teachings. Statues can be small decorations or larger than life.

ASIAN AMERICANS TODAY

More than 22 million Asian Americans live in the United States. This number continues to grow. Many Asian Americans live near cities on the West and East Coasts.

IMPORTANT ASIAN AMERICANS

Many Asian Americans have had an impact on US culture. Olivia Rodrigo is a famous singer, songwriter, and actress.

Olivia Rodrigo is Filipina American.

She is Filipina American. She starred in the Disney Channel show *Bizaardvark*. In 2021, her song "drivers license" became a number one hit. Rodrigo won big at the 2022 Grammy Awards. She won Best New Artist. "drivers license" earned her Best Pop Solo Performance. And she won best pop vocal album for her debut album, *SOUR*.

Jeremy Lin was the first Taiwanese American in the National Basketball Association (NBA). His career had a quiet start. But that changed in 2012. Lin's success on the court rocketed him to fame. He scored 38 points in a game against the Lakers. The period was known as "Linsanity." Lin became a powerful symbol for many Asian American viewers.

His success showed that Asian Americans could compete in basketball. Lin reflected on Linsanity 10 years later. “It was always, ‘Oh, he’s a good basketball player, but he’s Asian.’ . . . Society has always tried to say

Sunisa Lee

Sunisa Lee is an American gymnast. She won the all-around gymnastics gold medal at the Tokyo Olympics. She is the first Hmong American Olympian. The Hmong people came to the United States from parts of Thailand, Laos, and China. Many are refugees from the Vietnam War (1954–1975). Lee said, “[It] means a lot to the Hmong community . . . and to just be an inspiration to other Hmong people [means] a lot to me too.”

Karen Mizoguchi, “Sunisa Lee, First Hmong American Olympic Gymnast, Talks Achieving Her Dream and Being an Inspiration,” People, *July 9, 2021. http://people.com.*

Asians can't do this. Asians, you can't do that," he said. "What that moment meant was just being able to compete in the same court, in the same arena. And then to defeat and to overcome and to win."[7]

Kamala Harris served in the US Senate from 2017 to 2021. She became the first female US Vice President in 2021. She was the first Black American and the first South Asian American to hold the position. Her father immigrated from Jamaica. Her mother immigrated from India. In 2024, she ran for president. But she did not win the election.

EVERYDAY CHALLENGES

Today, Asian Americans are often treated as a monolith. This means they are grouped

Kamala Harris was the Democratic nominee for president in the 2024 election.

together under one label. This often leads to inequity. It erases diversity among Asian Americans. This is especially true for recent immigrants. They may struggle

The model minority myth includes stereotypes that all Asian Americans are good at school. This may not seem like a bad stereotype, but it can be harmful.

to adapt to American culture. They face language and class barriers.

Asian Americans may be seen as a model minority. The model minority myth is based on stereotypes. For example, Asian Americans are seen as high achievers. One stereotype is that all Asian Americans are good students. They're good at math and science. But this isn't true for all Asian Americans. Stereotypes may prevent students who need extra help from getting it.

The model minority myth has another downside. It pits Asian Americans against other ethnic groups. Some people use the myth to say racism does not exist. They may use it to defend discrimination against other groups. Gary Duong is Asian American. He discusses how the myth affects him and his husband, who is Black. "The whole idea of the 'model minority' is based on a myth," Duong says. "[It] is less a celebration of our accomplishments, and more of a convenient tool to mask ongoing discrimination and systemic inequality."[8]

EXPANDING ASIAN AMERICAN RIGHTS

May is Asian/Pacific American heritage month. The month celebrates Asian Americans and Pacific Islanders (AAPI). Pacific Islanders are another minority group in the United States. Their heritage comes from areas around the Pacific Ocean. These include Melanesia, Micronesia, and Polynesia. AAPI Heritage month gives time to reflect on the histories of these groups. Many communities host educational events to celebrate.

Hate crimes against AAPI people rose during the COVID-19 pandemic. The virus that caused the pandemic was first discovered in China. This caused some people to treat all Asian Americans poorly.

Hate crimes against Asian Americans rose in 2020. People across the country showed their support for Asian Americans.

The organization Stop AAPI Hate fights for AAPI communities. It provides resources to support communities affected by racism.

In 2022, New York City held its first annual AAPI Cultural and Heritage Parade.

Asian Americans have a long history in America. That history includes racism and stereotypes. It also includes success. Manjusha Kulkarni is the cofounder of Stop AAPI Hate. She says, "When you encourage hate, it's not like a genie in a bottle where you can pull it out and push it back in whenever you want. There's too much perpetuating these belief systems to make them go away."[9] Education is one way to fight hate. Learning about diversity helps people recognize other values and perspectives. Asian Americans are an important part of America's ethnic diversity.

GLOSSARY

boycott

the refusal to buy or participate in something until demands are met

confinement camps

places where prisoners or people who have been deemed dangerous are poorly housed and carefully watched

discrimination

treating a person or group worse than others due to differences

hate crime

crime or violence against individuals based on their identity

immigrated

moved from one country to another

prejudice

unfair bias or unfriendly feelings toward individuals or groups

racist

relating to racism, which is the systemic oppression of a racial group that creates an advantage for another racial group

stereotypes

oversimplified generalizations of people in a specific group

SOURCE NOTES

CHAPTER ONE: ASIAN AMERICAN HISTORY

1. Erika Lee, *The Making of Asian America*. Simon & Schuster, 2015, p. 4.

CHAPTER TWO: MANY CULTURES AND TRADITIONS

2. Quoted in Remy Tumin, "A Club Where Lion Dance and Traditions Take Root," *The New York Times*, January 22, 2017. www.nytimes.com.

3. Quoted in Harmeet Kaur, "Even in the US, South Asians Say Caste Has Proved Hard to Escape," *CNN*, September 8, 2020. www.cnn.com.

4. Quoted in Joe Heim, "Virginia's Vietnamese Americans Get Head Start on Celebrating Lunar New Year," *The Washington Post*, January 22, 2024. www.washingtonpost.com.

CHAPTER THREE: ASIAN AMERICAN RELIGIONS AND CELEBRATIONS

5. Quoted in "Eid al-Fitr: Reading Muslims Celebrate at Park Event," *BBC*, April 10, 2024. www.bbc.com.

6. Quoted in Sakshi Venkatraman, "The Percentage of Asian Americans Who Are Religious has Declined, New Study Finds," *NBC News*, October 11, 2023. www.nbcnews.com.

CHAPTER FOUR: ASIAN AMERICANS TODAY

7. Gary Duong, "You're Called a 'Model Minority' as an Asian American—Until They Decide You Aren't," *NPR*, May 30, 2022. www.npr.org.

8. The Associated Press, "More Than 9,000 Anti-Asian Incidents Have Been Reported Since the Pandemic Began," *NPR*, August 12, 2021. www.npr.org.

FOR FURTHER RESEARCH

BOOKS

Mary Boone, *Racial Injustice*. BrightPoint Press, 2023.

Racquel Foran, *A Look at Buddhism*. BrightPoint Press, 2024.

Naomi Hirahara, *We Are Here: 30 Inspiring Asian Americans and Pacific Islanders Who Have Shaped the United States*. RP Kids, 2022.

INTERNET SOURCES

"Asian Americans: Interactive Gallery," *PBS*, n.d. www.pbs.org.

"Chinese Poetry / Words from the Barracks," *Angel Island Immigration Station Foundation*, n.d. www.aiisf.org.

Léonie Shinn-Morris, "8 Things You Should Know About the Lucky Red Envelope," *Google Arts & Culture*, n.d. http://artsandculture.google.com.

WEBSITES

Asian Americans Collection: PBS Learning Media

http://pbslearningmedia.org/collection/asian-americans-pbs

This collection from PBS Learning Media includes a range of pictures and videos that showcase Asian American history in the United States.

Asian Art Museum

http://education.asianart.org

The Asian Art Museum website provides links to different activities relating to Asian American identities.

Stop AAPI Hate

http://stopaapihate.org

The Stop AAPI Hate website shares news, resources, and tools to fight hate against Asian Americans and Pacific Islanders.

INDEX

IMAGE CREDITS

Cover: © Creative Minds2/Shutterstock Images
5: © Kikujiarm/Shutterstock Images
7: © peeterv/iStockphoto
8: © Romix Image/Shutterstock Images
11: © rblfmr/Shutterstock Images
13: © SnapASkyline/Shutterstock Images
15: © EchoFree/Shutterstock Images
16: © National Park Service
21: © Library of Congress
23: © Garth Eliassen/Archive Photos/Getty Images
25: © SeventyFour/Shutterstock Images
26: © TD Dolci/iStockphoto
30: © IVASHstudio/Shutterstock Images
33: © Red Line Editorial
34: © Red Line Editorial
37: © MIA Studio/Shutterstock Images
40: © Odua Images/Shutterstock Images
42: © Clovera/Shutterstock Images
45: © cowardlion/Shutterstock Images
47: © Kathy Hutchins/Shutterstock Images
51: © Phil Mistry/Shutterstock Images
52: © Xavier Lorenzo/Shutterstock Images
55: © Sheila Fitzgerald/Shutterstock Images
56: © Ryan Rahman/Shutterstock Images

ABOUT THE AUTHOR

Keng Xiong is Hmong American. He is an editorial assistant from Andover, Minnesota. He has a bachelor's degree in English and creative writing. In his free time, he enjoys traveling and going to bookstores. He also loves trying out new foods from different cultures.